Lost

The Collapse of Morals in America: When Everything's for Sale

by

BRIAN TURNER

For permissions, inquiries, or bulk orders, please contact:
hi@heybbt.com
www.heybbt.com

First Edition
ISBN: 979-8-9931382-9-9

Printed in the United States of America

Table of Contents

right and wrong didn't disappear

Right and wrong didn't disappear. They just stopped trending.
We used to think right and wrong were permanent, like daylight and dark. Something you could count on, even if you sometimes stood in the shade.

---

back then

There was a time when right and wrong were printed on posters in every classroom. Red letters. Simple slogans. We repeated them until they felt like laws of nature.
"Just Say No." "Winners Never Quit." "Treat Others As You Want To Be Treated."
Not everyone lived by them, but they were there, like guardrails on a two-lane road. Even when we crossed the line, we knew the line existed.

There was a peace in knowing your neighbors, even if you didn't like them.
The streetlights came on and that was your curfew. Adults lowered their voices when children walked into the room.
You learned right and wrong not from laws, but from looks.

We had Saturday morning cartoons that ended with lessons.
Neighborhood block parties where somebody's mother knew your name.
Church bells on Sunday. The hum of the radio on the way to work.
Morals were not politics. They were manners. The effort to do right, even when no one was watching.

Even when the messages were simple or fake, they gave people something to aim for. The world seemed to agree that being good mattered, and that agreement gave people hope.

---

when it started to blur

Then the noise came. Cable. Talk shows. Shock value.
Rules bent for ratings, and every boundary we once drew started to look like entertainment.
We stopped asking what was true and started asking what would trend.
The heroes became complicated. The villains got sympathy.
And in that gray, we built a culture that believed you could do anything, as long as somebody was watching.

It wasn't evil that changed us. It was exhaustion.
We got tired of trying to be good when being loud paid better.

We traded discipline for dopamine and called it evolution.
The jobs multiplied, the bills grew, the screens filled our evenings, and slowly we convinced ourselves that the little rules no longer mattered.

There used to be silence. Not the kind you scroll through but the kind that made you think.
Then the noise arrived, commercials, headlines, notifications, and silence became the one thing we feared.

---

the gray area

Morality was never perfect; it was effort.
It was helping the next person. Leaving something better.
Breaking rules when necessary but remembering why they mattered.

Now, right and wrong are crowdsourced.
If enough people cheer for it, it becomes right.
If they cancel it, it becomes wrong.

Truth used to carry weight. Now it competes with sarcasm.
Empathy once felt like strength. Now it's branded as weakness.
Respect is optional. Kindness is content.

We claim to want honesty, but the moment it hurts, we label it hate.

The problem is not that morals disappeared. They may have been priced out.

And even now, we know something is off. We scroll through chaos, feeling it deeply.
We want to believe there is still good somewhere, but we do not know where to find it.
We accept the nonsense because rejecting it feels impossible.
At least back then, the world tried to sell us something decent, even if it was a lie.
Now we buy what breaks us and pretend it makes us free.

---

the mirror

Maybe we weren't as moral as we remember. Maybe we were just better at hiding it.
Pretending kept us respectable, and appearance passed for virtue.
But when the curtain fell, the truth was waiting.

Every generation blames the next for losing its way, but ours built the map.
We taught the world that image is currency and attention is power.
We built platforms that reward outrage, sold faith as fashion, and turned privacy into marketing.
We told kids they could be anything, but forgot to tell them what was worth being.

And the strangest part? We still call it progress.
Maybe, before we lost the world, we lost the will to keep trying.

---

where it began

If morality has a starting point, it might be somewhere small.
A classroom. A slogan. A promise printed on a glossy poster that said doing the right thing would always matter.
Maybe that is where we lost it, when the poster came down and the ad took its place.

Before morals collapsed on screens, they cracked in silence, in the homes, songs, and systems that stopped believing effort was enough.
Maybe it all started with something simple, a red-ink commandment we thought we understood.

Just Say No.

---

but before we move on

This book may exist because we still care.
Even if we've learned to laugh at everything, part of us still wants to believe in something.

We remember what it felt like to look up to people, even flawed ones.

To believe a better world could be built through effort, not algorithms.
That may be the only hope left, that enough of us still feel the loss and want to rebuild, one honest choice at a time.

lane 1 | parenting & education: when guidance disappeared

the first teachers

Morality begins long before the world teaches it.
It starts in the living room, in the voice that says "try again," in the look that says "you know better."
It starts with someone who loves you enough to correct you.

There was a time when the home was a classroom.
Parents were the first teachers. Teachers were the second parents.
Discipline was not cruelty.
It was care with structure.

The phrase 'because I said so' once meant something.
Now it is treated like oppression.
We used to teach children how to navigate authority.
Now we teach them how to avoid it.

The problem is not that kids have changed.
The truth is that adults surrendered.
We traded guidance for guilt.

We wanted to be liked more than we wanted to lead.

---

the home became a hotel

Parents used to raise their children.
Now, many just manage them.
Schedules, screens, and snacks, but never structure.
We have outsourced attention to algorithms and called it convenience.

Dinner tables used to be classrooms of conversation.
Now everyone eats in silence, together yet elsewhere.
Screens replaced stories.
Scrolling replaced sharing.

We tell ourselves we're too busy, but the truth is we're too distracted.
We forget that children don't just hear what we say.
They copy what we prioritize.
And right now, they are learning that busyness is love, and attention is optional.

---

the classroom lost its spine

Once, teachers commanded respect by presence alone.
A look was enough to restore order.

Now, classrooms have become battlegrounds of blame.
Parents blame teachers.
Teachers fear parents.
And children learn that authority is negotiable.

Education used to shape character.
Now it shapes comfort.
We protect children from every discomfort except ignorance.
We reward effort with equality, not excellence.

We've raised a generation that believes correction is cruelty and failure is trauma.
But growth never came from comfort.
It came from falling short and standing back up, lessons we have replaced with leniency.

---

the confusion of curriculum

Somewhere along the way, education stopped asking what children need to learn and started asking what adults want to argue about.
Morality became political.
Truth became optional.

We replaced timeless principles with temporary positions.
We stopped teaching wisdom and started teaching opinions.
There was a time when history humbled us.
Now it divides us.

We are so busy rewriting it that we forgot to learn from it.

Children aren't confused because they're young. They are confused because the adults are dishonest. When truth depends on who's talking, right and wrong lose meaning.

---

the every-child-is-right era

We used to teach children that effort matters.
Now we teach them that feelings do.
We have created a generation allergic to disappointment and addicted to validation.

Trophies used to symbolize achievement.
Now they symbolize attendance.
Even in sports, the last-place effort still matters most; everyone gets one.
Losing used to build character.
Now it builds complaints.
We teach kids that showing up is enough, then wonder why resilience disappears when life stops handing out medals.

When everyone wins, no one learns how to lose.
And when no one learns how to lose, no one learns how to grow.

Accountability used to build confidence.
Now avoidance builds anxiety.

We're raising kids to believe they can be anything but without the character to become someone.

---

what we gained / what we lost

gains

- Awareness of emotional needs

- Inclusion and sensitivity

- Platforms for new voices in education

---

losses

- Respect for authority

- The link between discipline and love

- The belief that truth is not personal

---

the bridge | to the culture

Morality used to start at home and echo in schools. Now it starts on screens and echoes in silence. Even in sports, once a sanctuary of lessons in teamwork, grit, and humility, we've softened the

scoreboards and silenced the consequences.
we have softened the scoreboards and silenced the
consequences.

A child's compass is set by what the adults repeat.
For the first time, adults are unsure which direction
is north.

What happens when guidance disappears?
The screen takes its place.
That is where the next lane begins.

lane 2 | tv, cartoons & movies: when family meant something

when the screen taught us right and wrong

Before phones became mirrors, the television was our teacher.
We didn't just watch shows. We learned from them.
There were no algorithms or endless feeds, only stories with a beginning, a middle, and a lesson.

You could turn on *The Cosby Show*, *Family Matters*, *Full House*, or *The Fresh Prince of Bel-Air* and feel like you were being raised alongside them.
Parents weren't perfect, but they were present.
They taught discipline and empathy.
The kids made mistakes, but they learned and grew.
Every episode ended with resolution, not chaos.

Even the cartoons carried codes of honor.
He-Man taught courage and restraint.
Transformers preached loyalty and sacrifice.
G.I. Joe closed each episode with the line, "Knowing is half the battle."
Even Thundercats and Voltron taught teamwork, bravery, and unity.

Those shows didn't just entertain us. They formed us.
They told us good mattered, even when life didn't seem fair.
They made morality aspirational.

---

the black family on screen

For Black America, those shows weren't just stories. They were strategy.
The Cosby Show wasn't about sweaters. It was about structure.
A doctor and a lawyer raising children who were respectful, curious, and loved them back.
It showed a version of life we wanted to believe was possible.

Then came *A Different World*, showing college life with pride and purpose.
Family Matters gave us consistency and love.
The *Fresh Prince of Bel Air* mixed humor with depth. It explored class, pain, abandonment, and growth.
Even when the jokes hit, the message hit harder.
Family still mattered, no matter how complicated it looked.

Those shows made Black love look strong, not scandalous.
They made fatherhood look sacred, not optional.

They made community look like something worth protecting.

Now, it feels different.
Representation still exists, but respect feels optional.
We went from showing excellence to showcasing chaos.
The mirror cracked, and the image shifted. We became caricatures of the families we once aspired to be.

---

when the messages started to blur

Then came the turning point: reality TV.
What started as curiosity became conditioning.

The Real World sold conflict as connection.
Jerry Springer made dysfunction daytime entertainment.
Then *Flavor of Love*, *Keeping Up With the Kardashians*, and *Love & Hip Hop* turned chaos into currency.
We started celebrating the things that used to embarrass us.
Arguments, betrayal, and fighting became entertainment.

We didn't just laugh at the madness.
We started mimicking it.
We learned that drama pays.
That humiliation can go viral.

That family could be a brand if you were loud enough.

The lesson was no longer "do better."
It was "get noticed."

---

the collapse of innocence

Cartoons changed, too.
They stopped teaching. They started teasing.
Sarcasm replaced sincerity.
Heroes became antiheroes.
Villains became misunderstood.
The lines blurred until no one was right or wrong, only famous or forgotten.

You can see it in the stories.
The Simpsons turned family into farce.
South Park made mockery the message.
Even children's shows began slipping in cynicism, with quick jokes that taught cleverness instead of kindness.
Movies followed the same script.
Batman stopped being a symbol of justice and became a study in trauma.
The Joker became the philosopher.
Disney traded lessons for legacy sequels and nostalgia with no new wisdom.
We went from rooting for heroes to relating to villains.

I still remember sitting in that dark theater watching *Transformers: The Movie* and crying when Optimus Prime died.
It wasn't just a cartoon.
It was a lesson about sacrifice, leadership, and what happens when good loses.
We were invested in good.
We cared if it won.

Movies like *The Lion King*, *Karate Kid*, *Rocky*, and *Remember the Titans* evoked a sense of nobility.
They made us believe discipline, teamwork, and sacrifice mattered.
Now the stories feel different.
The antihero replaced the role model.
We root for revenge, not redemption.
We cheer for survival, not transformation.

Ask yourself, are there any shows left that teach good values?
And if there are, are they consistent enough to compete with the noise?

---

the mirror effect

Screens used to reflect what we wanted to become.
Now they reflect what we already tolerate.
We watch people fall apart and call it reality.
We laugh at dysfunction until we start living it.
And when you see enough chaos, peace starts to look fake.

The family that once gathered around one television now sits in silence, each person staring at their own screen.
We no longer learn lessons together; we consume opinions alone.
What once united us as viewers now divides us as identities.
The screen doesn't raise children anymore. It raises reactions.

---

gains

- Representation across cultures and stories.

- Art that finally told the truth about pain.

- Voices that were once silent now have microphones.

---

losses

- Shared moral imagination.

- The concept of family as foundation.

- Hope as a narrative ending.

- The belief that innocence deserves protection.

- The idea that right and wrong were worth showing, even when unpopular.

---

bridge | from screens to systems

Television once shaped the soul.
Now it sells it.
When storytellers lost their compass, corporations picked up the pen.
They learned that moral confusion is profitable and predictable.
The stories stopped asking who we are and started deciding what we buy.

And when the screen became the parent, the soundtrack followed.

lane 3 | music: the soundtrack of the shift

when the songs had meaning

There was a time when music was a map.
Every neighborhood had an anthem that made people feel seen.
We sang about love, hope, and struggle because it reminded us who we were.
Even when life was hard, the songs said we still had a chance.

You could turn on the radio and hear Michael sing *"Man in the Mirror."*
Whitney belting out *"Greatest Love of All."*
Public Enemy warning, *"Don't Believe the Hype."*
We Are the World played like a national prayer.
The melody carried unity. The message carried accountability.
Artists talked about building, believing, surviving.
The beat wasn't just rhythm. It was responsibility.

Even hip-hop, born in struggle, carried its own code.
You could feel the pride in *Self Destruction* and *We're All in the Same Gang*.
The lyrics admitted pain but pointed toward progress.
The rappers who talked about hustling wanted out, not applause.

They rhymed about the danger, not the lifestyle.
They saw themselves as reporters, not recruiters.

Music didn't just reflect life. It corrected it.

---

when the message changed

Somewhere between the studio and the algorithm, purpose got traded for performance.
The industry learned that pain sells faster than peace.
Labels chased shock over soul, and every generation started humming its own disillusionment.

The beats got darker. The hooks got emptier.
We went from "Self Destruction" to "Mask Off."
From Marvin Gaye asking *What's Going On* to choruses celebrating not caring at all.
Even love songs sound tired now, more transaction than tenderness.
Music stopped lifting us. It started describing our collapse.

Rappers used to rap about selling drugs to survive.
Now they rap about using them to feel alive.
The hustler's dream of escape turned into the addict's anthem of escape from himself.
We used to admire ambition. Now we applaud apathy.

---

the female voice

There was a time when women on the mic carried a different kind of power.
Queen Latifah asked, *"Who you callin' a b***?"*
Lauryn Hill preached balance and soul.
MC Lyte, Missy, Salt-N-Pepa: bold, playful, confident, but still building.
They didn't have to show skin to show strength.

Now the freedom they fought for exists, but the message has changed.
What was once empowerment turned into exposure.
Image became the art.
Lyrics became leverage.
It's not that women lost power — they were forced to monetize it.
Sex sells because everything does.

The result? A generation of girls learning that validation is volume.
That worth is measured in followers, not foundation.
And when every chorus repeats it enough, belief becomes behavior.

---

the economics of emotion

When the internet took control, everything sped up.
Art stopped aging. It just refreshed.
Songs became content.
Artists became algorithms.

The machine learned our sadness and sold it back to us.

Streams replaced record sales, and virality replaced vision.
A song no longer needed meaning. It just needed fifteen seconds of attention.
We lost patience for the slow burn of soul.
The moral of the story no longer needed a bridge, just a beat drop.

Pain became a product, and the charts turned into confessionals with no redemption arc.
Even joy sounds borrowed now, the rhythm of a world pretending to dance while drowning.

---

the reflection

There's nothing wrong with evolution.
Art should change.
But somewhere, the purpose slipped.
Music used to heal the wound. Now it describes it.
And every time we dance to despair, we make it harder to imagine joy.

Maybe that's the quiet tragedy:
we traded inspiration for identification.
We stopped asking what a song stood for and started asking how it made us feel, even if that feeling was empty.

The melodies got louder as the message got smaller.
And the world learned to hum its heartbreak in harmony.

---

gains

- Creative freedom.

- Global voices without gatekeepers.

- Honesty about pain.

- New technology that gave anyone a mic.

---

losses

- Unity.

- Moral melody.

- The belief that music could make us better, not just mirror the worst.

- The power of message over metrics.

- The sound of hope itself.

the echo

I can't listen to most of it anymore.
Not because I'm old, but because I remember when
music tried to heal.
When a song could make a broken world believe
again.

Now it reminds me that we stopped trying.
Once the soundtrack shifted, the slogans never
stood a chance.
'Just Say No' would be the first to fall.

lane 4 | drugs: from "just say no" to "everybody does it"

the promise

By the time the chorus changed, the classroom was ready for new commandments.

We sat on hard plastic chairs under fluorescent lights while a police officer in mirrored sunglasses warned that one bad choice could ruin our lives.
The posters were everywhere: a red circle, a slash through white powder.
The D.A.R.E. T-shirts were trophies, proof that we knew better.
Saying *no* felt like a superpower.

It was the last time America tried to make morality sound cool.
Commercials preached discipline. Teachers handed out stickers shaped like stop signs.
Even the music joined in, catchy and bright, reminding us that clean was good and high was hell.
We believed it, mostly.
Not because we understood addiction, but because the message was simple: good people stayed clear, bad people fell apart.

For a moment, it felt like the country agreed on something.

---

the illusion of control

But the story behind the slogans was never clean. While kids in suburbs wore D.A.R.E. shirts, entire neighborhoods were being handcuffed by policy. The same government that said 'Just Say No' also said 'Three Strikes and You're Out.'
Moral lessons became sentencing guidelines.

The kids who grew up believing those slogans got older and realized the campaign had another purpose.
The same voices that preached purity built a pipeline from the classroom to the courthouse.
The Clinton crime bill promised safety and delivered silence. Neighborhoods emptied of fathers and brothers who never got a second chance.
Just Say No turned into *Just Lock Them Up.*
It was the same message of control, only written in fine print.
When trust breaks that early, every moral message after sounds like marketing.
And when the truth came out, an entire generation stopped trusting the word *morals* altogether.

Addiction was a headline, not a health issue.
Crack addicts went to prison.
Cocaine users went to rehab.

And the dealers? They were branded as monsters.
Faces on the evening news, symbols of decay.
Some were victims of the same system that created
the hunger they fed.
Some were hustlers trying to survive a world that
offered them nothing else.
But the message was the same: lock them up,
throw away the key, and call it justice.
The supply chain of pain had many hands, but only
one group paid the full price.
Morality was color-coded, and justice looked like
judgment dressed as virtue.

We thought we were saving souls.
Mostly, we were saving appearances.

the turn

Then the script flipped.
In came the pharmacies, the pills with friendly
names, the commercials that promised peace in
thirty seconds.
Doctors replaced dealers. Prescriptions replaced
warnings.
We didn't end the drug era. We privatized it.

Suddenly, it was fine to need a pill.
Fine to take something for sleep, for calm, for focus,
for pain.
Fine to sell relief as a brand.
Bottles lined bathroom counters like trophies of

survival.
We just stopped calling it addiction.

When marijuana shops opened on corners once patrolled for possession, people called it progress.
And maybe some of it was.
But something subtle changed. The fear turned fashionable.
Every high had a hashtag.
Every escape came with better marketing.

We didn't fix addiction.
We just found better lighting for it.

---

the reflection

Maybe that's what moral collapse looks like: not rebellion, but rebranding.
The drugs changed, but the need stayed the same.
We're still running from pain, only now we call it self-care.
We post our anxiety, romanticize our trauma, and celebrate survival as if it were balance.

When everything hurts, intoxication feels like honesty.
People film overdoses, edit tragedy into content, add background music, and call it awareness.
We used to whisper about the people who lost control.
Now we scroll past them.

The old slogans told us to stay away.
The new culture tells us to find ourselves in the fog.
Somewhere along the way, clarity stopped being
cool.

---

gains

- Honest conversation about mental health.

- Compassion for people fighting addiction.

- Reform that treats dependency as disease, not crime.

losses

- The belief that restraint has value.

- The understanding that peace is earned, not prescribed.

- The idea that clear minds build clear lives.

---

the echo

We used to fear losing our minds.
Now we call it finding ourselves.

Somewhere between the high and the numb, the soundtrack changed too.

lane 5 | monopolies: when competition meant character

the dream we were sold

For generations, we were told that America was a place where anyone could win.
If you worked hard, you earned your share.
If you stayed loyal, you were rewarded.
The moral code was simple: play fair, do right, and you'd have a shot.

People came from everywhere believing in that promise.
They believed in the idea that effort mattered more than inheritance.
That character was the currency of success.
We called it the American Dream, but it was more than a dream. It was a belief system.
It told us that opportunity was a shared language, not a corporate secret.

For a while, that faith held us together.
Competition built pride.
Success felt earned, not engineered.
And when we lost, we still believed in the rules.

But the dream changed.
It became a pitch, a product sold to the next generation with the price tag hidden.
Somewhere between the commercials and the contracts, morality got rewritten.
Right and wrong weren't the question anymore.
Only winning was.

---

when competition built character

There was a time when competition meant something sacred.
You opened your shop early, swept the sidewalk, and let your work speak for you.
Your name was your brand. Your word was your warranty.
Every business, builder, and craftsman was judged by how well they served people, not shareholders.

We were taught that hard work built character, and character built community.
A handshake mattered.
You could lose a sale and still keep your soul.
The marketplace felt human, not mechanical.
Competition was moral. It forced you to be better, not just bigger.

---

the rise of control

Then the rules changed.
The few learned that control was easier than character.
If you couldn't outwork your rival, you bought them.
If you couldn't compete, you consolidated.
If you couldn't innovate, you acquired.

The great mergers began quietly.
Banks devoured banks.
Pharmacies became grocery stores, which became insurance companies.
Media companies swallowed each other until every headline sounded the same.
Technology promised freedom but delivered dependency.
The same five corporations began deciding what we see, what we buy, and what we believe.

And behind the scenes, the music labels moved the same way.
A handful of conglomerates now control nearly every voice on the radio, every playlist on the platforms, every sound that gets to define a generation.
It's not just the notes that are owned. It's the message.
Once, music told the truth of the streets. Now it tells the story of the sponsors.
The rebellion got licensed. The struggle got rebranded. The profit stayed the same.

There was a time when this kind of dominance wasn't just discouraged, it was dismantled.

The antitrust era treated monopolies as moral failures, not business triumphs.
When Microsoft was accused of crushing competition in the 1990s, the outrage wasn't about software; it was about fairness.
We understood that when one player owns the whole game, everyone else stops playing.
Now, those same tactics are celebrated as strategy.
We reward the very behavior we used to regulate.

We once broke up giants for the good of the people.
AT&T's empire was split so voices could compete.
Standard Oil was shattered so progress could breathe.
Microsoft was warned that power without restraint would poison innovation.
Now, Amazon builds what it wants.
Google owns the gate to knowledge.
Meta shapes the mood of nations.
And the same record companies that once fought for artists now fight for algorithms.

---

the loyalty contract

There was a time when companies didn't just employ people, they protected them.
If you gave thirty years of your life, they gave thirty more in return.
Pensions were promises.
They said, "We'll take care of you when you can't

take care of yourself."
That wasn't charity. It was morality in motion.

Then the ledger changed.
Retirement became a risk instead of a reward.
Pensions vanished, replaced by personal plans and shifting markets.
Responsibility moved from the boardroom to the break room.
The message was clear: you're on your own now.

And the irony?
These companies made more money than ever.
They broke the contract not because they had to, but because they could.
The move toward 401(k)s, gig work, and "you're on your own" culture symbolized the shift from community capitalism to survival capitalism.
And survival has no morals.

That's when loyalty died.
And once loyalty died, everything else was for sale.

---

capitalism's conversion

Then we redefined capitalism.
It shifted its focus from creation to consumption.
The purpose wasn't to build anymore; it was to dominate.
Companies started calling greed strategy.
Stock prices became morality.
As long as the line went up, the story stayed good.

But the numbers lied.
They rose on the backs of people whose pensions disappeared, whose hours doubled, whose savings vanished in systems they didn't design.
It wasn't survival of the fittest anymore.
It was survival of the richest.

We didn't lose faith in capitalism.
Capitalism lost faith in us.

---

the illusion of choice

We still think we're choosing.
We just choose between versions of the same owner.
Different logos, same leaders.
Different apps, same algorithms.

We scroll through options like free people, but every click feeds the same system.
Fast food, fashion, film, finance: everything funnels to a handful of hands.
The shelves look full, but the source is small.
Freedom became a product feature, not a principle.

The moral collapse here isn't just greed.
It's disconnection.
When no one knows who is responsible, no one feels responsible.
And when profit has no face, neither does accountability.

when the values vanished

There was a time when success had to serve.
You built trust before you built scale.
Companies wanted loyalty, not data.
They earned it through service, not surveillance.

Now, success means dominance.
The moral question changed from "Is it right?" to
"Does it convert?"
We stopped asking what things are worth.
We started asking what they're worth to the market.

Community became consumer base.
Loyalty became lifetime value.
We built systems so efficient they forgot to be
human.
The invisible hands of the market no longer lift, they
take.

We even wrote books about it.
We told ourselves the great companies were built to
last.
That success came from purpose, vision, and values.
But decades later, those same brands were gutted,
sold, and spun off.
The truth wasn't that the values failed. It's that the
markets stopped rewarding them.

the human cost

Small towns hollowed out.
Local stores were replaced by warehouses and delivery trucks.
The corner diner where everyone knew your name became another vacant lot.
We replaced the cashier with a code, the craftsman with a chain, and the face with a function.

The cost wasn't just jobs.
It was meaning.
It was knowing who you were working for and who was working for you.
Now everyone works for the feed.

We traded proximity for productivity, and nobody can find home anymore.

---

the dream undone

We used to compete to build.
Now we compete to own.
When ownership replaces purpose, the dream collapses from the inside.
The rat race isn't the system, it's the symptom.
We're running faster inside a machine we no longer control.
The louder it hums, the quieter our conscience gets.

---

gains

- Efficiency that moves at the speed of thought

- Innovation that shrinks the world

- Access that once belonged only to a few

---

losses

- Character as a business model

- Accountability as a standard

- The pride of competing fairly and building faithfully

- The belief that success should serve people, not consume them

---

the bridge | from power to permission

Monopolies don't just own markets. They own narratives.
Once they controlled money, they began controlling the message.
They decide who gets seen, who gets silenced, what rises, and what disappears.
And the people in power learned to play along.

What started as competition for customers became competition for control.
From here, morality no longer belongs to the people. It belongs to those who can afford it.

That is where the next lane begins.

lane 6 | politics & power: when service became strategy

the purpose of politics

There was a time when politics meant service.
Leadership was supposed to be moral labor, the responsibility of protecting people, not manipulating them.
Your word was your reputation, and your reputation was public record.
A leader's character was as important as their policy.

The system was not perfect, but it felt like it believed in itself.
There were guardrails, rules, limits, and expectations.
Government of the people, by the people, and for the people was not a slogan. It was a standard.
It implied accountability. It implied that people mattered.

We believed that good leadership could rise above bad moments.
That truth could still steady the country when everything else shook.
It wasn't naïve. It was faith, and faith was a kind of morality.

the turn to performance

Then politics became a stage.
Policy turned into publicity.
The press conference replaced the plan.
Leaders stopped governing the nation and started managing narratives.

Every appearance was calculated.
Every apology rehearsed.
Every value was tested by polling before it was spoken aloud.
The job was not to serve anymore. It was to trend.

We stopped electing visionaries and started hiring influencers.
Sincerity became a brand.
Empathy became a caption.
And every move, even decency, became strategy.

the money machine

Somewhere along the way, power stopped being earned and started being sponsored.
Lobbyists wrote the laws.
Donors wrote the priorities.
Corporations funded both sides and called it democracy.

Campaigns turned into marketing agencies, and elections became billion-dollar ad spends.
Every policy had a price tag.
Every position had a buyer.
Public service became private gain.

The pipeline between Wall Street and Washington became so efficient they stopped pretending it was separate.
Money did not just influence power. It became the only language power could understand.

---

from scandal to strategy

There was a time when scandal meant shame.
A lie could end a career.
Now it starts a fundraising campaign.

Outrage is not a crisis anymore. It is a business model.
The moral shock that once humbled leaders now trends for twenty-four hours before the next distraction arrives.
Integrity became negotiable.
Hypocrisy became tradition.
We learned to reward the best performer, not the most principled.

Every apology comes with merch.
Every lie has a focus group.

---

the blurred lines of law and business

I remember studying finance in college.
Back then, balancing the budget mattered.
It was more than arithmetic. It was accountability.
We believed that numbers told the truth.
That discipline was patriotic.

Insider trading was a crime, not a career path.
It may have been a lie, but it felt like there were still
rules, and that mattered.
Transparency was expected, not optional.
But somewhere between Wall Street's bailout and
Washington's debt ceiling, the numbers became
political.

Now the deficit is a shrug.
The national debt grows like a rumor, too large to
measure, too abstract to fix.
We used to fake balance sheets. Now we fake
balance itself.
Fiscal restraint became political suicide.
The math stopped adding up because the morality
disappeared with it.

---

capitalism's favorite partner

Capitalism did not corrupt politics. It recruited it.
Corporate money does not lobby anymore. It
legislates.
It writes the bills, funds the campaigns, and owns
the airwaves that shape how we see both.

The government stopped guarding fairness and started managing optics.
It protects profits, not people.
It enforces narratives, not laws.
And the moral duty to serve was rewritten as a strategy to survive.

Capitalism found its perfect accomplice in government.
One controls the market. The other controls the message.

---

the politics of distraction

When leadership failed, entertainment stepped in.
We turned the republic into reality TV.
Every issue became a sideshow.
Every citizen became a spectator.

They managed to turn everything into a political debate.
Masks, vaccines, pronouns, even empathy.
It isn't governance anymore. It's a circus.
A televised feud where facts are props and outrage is applause.

The more divided the people, the safer the powerful.
Outrage became an industry. Confusion became currency.
We no longer argue ideas. We perform them.
And every performance keeps us distracted while the same hands pull the same strings.

The moral center is not left or right. It is lost.

---

the cost of disillusionment

People stopped believing in government because government stopped believing in people.
Cynicism became self-defense.
Hopelessness spread faster than inflation.

We used to measure decline in dollars.
Now we measure it in faith, and there is nothing left in the account.
When you don't trust the rules, you stop playing the game.
That is when moral collapse becomes permanent.
Not when the laws fail, but when belief does.

---

gains

- Transparency tools, watchdog journalism, and digital activism

- Citizens can now see the game, even if they cannot win it

---

losses

- Integrity as an expectation

- Truth as a public resource

- The idea that public office is public service

---

the bridge | from politics to the marketplace

Power learned to perform, and the market learned
to reward it.
When leadership became theater, everything else
became inventory.
From here, morality is not debated. It is priced.
That is where the next lane begins.

lane 7 | the selling of the soul: when everything became for sale

the price of everything

There was a time when not everything had a price.
Some things were sacred.
Love, truth, loyalty, and dignity belonged to the human part of life, not the market.

But somewhere along the way, the line disappeared.
The sacred became negotiable.
The meaningful became measurable.
Everything found a buyer.

We started treating attention like currency, affection like content, and authenticity like inventory.
The question stopped being "What do you believe in?"
It became "What can you sell?"

The American Dream turned from aspiration into a product.
It used to mean freedom and purpose.
Now it means reach and profit.
We no longer chase meaning. We chase monetization.

from purpose to profit

Once, value came from what something stood for.
Now it comes from what it can earn.
We stopped building legacies and started building
followings.
The new morality is visibility.

The influencer replaced the leader.
The algorithm replaced the mentor.
The message became whatever kept the feed alive.

We do not ask what is true anymore.
We ask what will trend.
A soul used to be measured by conviction.
Now it is measured by conversions.

sex and the illusion of power

We used to be too shy to show our faces on camera.
Now we perform for strangers just to feel seen.
What we once hid to protect our dignity, we now
reveal to prove our worth.

At first, it was harmless.
A bikini photo. A wink. A tease.
A way to say, look at me, I matter too.
But attention is a gateway drug.
And the dollar always asks for a little more.

We tell ourselves it is just expression, just control, just independence.
But slowly, the line moves.
We start where it feels safe and end wherever the money is willing to take us.
The camera becomes confession.
The likes become validation.
The audience becomes God.

Prostitution was once whispered about in shame.
Now it is branded as empowerment.
Desire became content.
Love became leverage.
Affection turned into an audience.

We told ourselves it was freedom, but it was just another hustle.
OnlyFans, subscriptions, private links, and intimacy now have an interface.
The oldest profession found its newest platform.
It is not shameful anymore. It is scalable.

But the illusion of power is loneliness in disguise.
For every person selling control, there is another buying comfort.
For every creator chasing attention, there is an emptiness waiting when the lights go off.
Even desire learned to scale, and in doing so, it lost its soul.

The problem is not that people sell their bodies.
It is that the world taught them their worth is only marketable through them.

We do not crave connection anymore. We crave confirmation.
And when everything becomes a performance, nobody remembers what it feels like to be touched without being watched.

---

the gospel of gambling

There was a time when gambling lived in the shadows.
Casinos were sin cities, not sponsorships.
Now it is the face of sports.

You can't watch a game without seeing the odds.
You can't dream without seeing the bet.
Risk used to be a warning. Now it is a brand.

The same dopamine once reserved for dreams now powers the apps that drain them.
Even hope became a commodity.
We buy the chance to win back the life we already lost.

We used to say don't gamble with your future.
Now we gamble to afford it.

---

the culture of constant promotion

Everyone is selling something now.
Products, personalities, philosophies.

Even the idea of not selling has become its own marketing strategy.

Hustle became religion.
Self-worth became a pitch deck.
The words grind and brand sound the same in the mouth of exhaustion.

We used to work to live.
Now we work to be seen working.
Authenticity became the most profitable lie.
The truth doesn't need filters, but the truth doesn't get followers either.

We sold ambition as empowerment and burnout as success.
We're promoting ourselves into oblivion.

---

the myth of freedom

We are told we are freer than ever.
But freedom that must be performed is not freedom at all.
Every post is a product. Every opinion is data.
We are no longer the audience. We are the inventory.

Every click, every like, every search is sold to the same machine that claims to serve us.
Our identities are packaged and sold back to us through ads promising individuality.

We didn't lose our souls to sin.
We leased them to systems.

We rent our homes, our cars, our time, our identities.
The new chains are invisible, but the weight is the same.

---

the human toll

We're the most connected generation in history and the loneliest one, too.
We have access to everything but intimacy with nothing.
We scroll past suffering, sell our sadness, and package our pain for engagement.

The body, the mind, the truth, all for rent.
The final cost of selling everything is that we forget what cannot be bought.

Depression in the age of abundance.
Anxiety in the age of access.
Loneliness in the crowd of a billion voices.
We traded the soul for the screen, and the screen never loved us back.

---

gains

- Access for the unheard

- Platforms for the creative

- A chance for independence that once required permission

---

losses

- Meaning as a measure of success

- Love as something unquantifiable

- The belief that everything valuable cannot be monetized

---

the bridge | back to belief

When everything has been sold, what is left to save?
We have turned value into vanity and freedom into finance.
But there are still a few things the market cannot reach.
The whisper of conscience.
The stillness of truth.
The quiet peace of knowing you did right when no one was watching.

The world can sell almost anything now, but it still cannot buy the soul back.
Maybe that's not a beginning at all.
Maybe it is the last thing left unbroken.

lane 8 | the people: when right stopped feeling right

the reflection in the mirror

Every system we blame learned from us.
The market mirrors our desires.
The screen mirrors our impulses.
Politics mirrors our excuses.

Morality did not vanish.
We just stopped wanting to carry it.
It felt heavy. It felt slow. It got in the way of being seen.

We traded conviction for comfort, and then called it authenticity.
The world did not lose its morals.
We sold them back to ourselves at a discount.

the celebration of wrong

We used to hide bad behavior. Now we post it.
Shame once sent us inward. Now it sends us viral.
Disrespect trends faster than integrity.
Scandal sells better than sincerity.

There was a time when you would lower your voice while cursing in public.
Now we film ourselves doing it for views.

We stopped calling things wrong and started calling them content.
Every confession is a performance.
Every downfall is a debut.
We reward the breakdown before we encourage the rebuild.

---

the empathy drought

We hear everything and listen to nothing.
Outrage replaced understanding.
Everyone is broadcasting. No one is witnessing.

Kindness feels corny.
Patience feels weak.
Empathy feels outdated.

We measure morality by alignment, not compassion.
We do not ask who is hurting. We ask who you're with.

---

the rise of self over soul

We were told to love ourselves. Somewhere we learned to worship ourselves.

'Do you' replaced 'do good.'
Confidence became a costume for character.

The self-help we needed turned into self-promotion.
We built personal brands and neglected personal growth.
Image became identity.
Influence became virtue.
The soul went quiet in the noise.

---

the loss of consequence

There was a time when being wrong carried weight.
Now it carries reach.
Delete, rebrand, relaunch.

We fear being canceled more than being corrupt.
We are terrified of judgment but unbothered by guilt.
When crowds decide what is right, right becomes temporary.
Truth becomes relative.
Consequence disappears.

---

the addiction to permission

We wait for likes to approve what conscience already answered.
We crowdsource courage and rent conviction by the weekend.

We know when we've crossed the line. We scroll until someone tells us we didn't.

---

the illusion of progress

We call it evolution because it moves fast.
But speed is not growth.
Noise is not wisdom.

Every new freedom arrives without a framework and leaves us emptier than before.
We mastered expression and forgot restraint.
We can do almost anything now. We still don't know what's worth doing.

---

the quiet ones

There are still people doing right. They just don't trend.
They forgive without cameras.
They give without hashtags.
They hold their promises in small rooms where no one claps.

Goodness has gone underground.
Small. Steady. Stubborn.
Maybe that's where revival always begins.

---

gains

- Awareness of our contradictions

- Platforms where truth can travel if we let it

- Language for wounds we used to hide

---

losses

- Shame as a teacher

- Empathy as instinct

- Truth as a compass

---

the bridge | from people to proof

A nation becomes what its people reward.
We rewarded noise, and we received it back as news.
We rewarded performance, and we received it back as truth.

If the mirror is cloudy, the lens will be worse.
From here, the story moves to the filter itself, where reality is edited, facts are tribal, and lies arrive looking honest.

That's where the next lane begins.

lane 9 | truth & media: the death of reality

the credibility we trusted

There was a time when truth had a face.
When the evening news came from voices that sounded like fathers and uncles.
You could turn on the television and feel informed, not infected.
Facts were steady. Headlines were brief.
News was a duty, not an industry.

Anchors like Walter Cronkite, Peter Jennings, Tom Brokaw, and Barbara Walters carried the weight of honesty.
They did not chase clicks. They carried calm.
The role of journalism was to translate chaos into clarity, not to amplify the noise.
The job was to tell the truth, even when it hurt.
For a while, that was enough.

the rise of the 24-hour cycle

Then came the clock that never stopped.
CNN, Fox, and MSNBC turned information into entertainment.
The news did not wait to be verified. It just needed

to be first.
Stories became speculation, and speculation became story.
The ticker at the bottom of the screen replaced the patience we once had for facts.
The line between urgency and manipulation blurred.

Fear sells. Outrage retains.
The formula worked too well to ignore.
Every crisis became a cliffhanger.
Every tragedy became a segment.
We learned to crave catastrophe.
We stopped watching for clarity and started watching for comfort.

Truth became the casualty of attention.

---

when headlines replaced honesty

Somewhere between the anchor desk and the algorithm, the mission changed.
Accuracy lost to engagement.
Integrity bowed to influence.
The public stopped reading full stories and started reacting to headlines.
Newsrooms learned to phrase every truth as a question and every lie as a possibility.
It wasn't deception. It was strategy.
And strategy paid better.

Clicks became currency.
Rage became retention.
We no longer looked for the truth.
We scrolled until we found the version that fit our bias.
Reality splintered into algorithms.
Everyone got their own version of the same event, curated to confirm what they already believed.
We didn't just lose common ground. We lost a common reality.

---

the entertainment of outrage

Talk shows turned debate into theater.
Panelists performed conflict.
Hosts interrupted, laughed, and shouted over facts.
The louder the voice, the higher the rating.
The audience was not asked to think, only to pick a side.

We used to believe the news was a mirror.
Now it is a mood.
If it doesn't make us feel something, we scroll past it.
If it challenges us, we call it bias.
The press stopped reporting what happened and started shaping what people should feel about it.

We learned to trust personalities instead of principles.
Charisma replaced credibility.

The journalist became the brand.
The story became the spin.

---

the social experiment

Then came social media, the final merger between opinion and identity.
Everyone became a broadcaster.
Everyone became an expert.
Truth became a popularity contest.
If enough people shared it, it must be real.

The timeline turned into a courtroom with no judge.
Facts had no defense.
Rumors traveled faster than retractions.
We rewarded the clever over the correct, the viral over the verified.

Even journalists began competing with influencers.
Posts replaced reporting.
Verification became a blue check, not a standard.
We didn't just consume the news anymore. We became it.

---

the illusion of independence

For a while, it looked like the system had finally cracked.
Independent voices were rising on YouTube and podcasts, armed with laptops and conviction.

They spoke the truth the networks would not touch.
They fact-checked the fact-checkers.
They exposed what the headlines buried.

At first, it felt like a revolution.
Ordinary people with microphones were
challenging billion-dollar studios.
The underdogs were winning views.
The public was listening again.

But then came the algorithm.
The same machine that elevated them began to
own them.
Truth became performance again, just on a
different stage.
They learned that outrage drives clicks, that drama
feeds the feed.
That moral clarity does not monetize as well as
controversy.

The more influence they gained, the more the
mainstream noticed.
And one by one, the independents got offers.
Partnerships. Sponsorships. Platforms.
The system bought what it could not silence.
The same hands that once filtered the truth
through television now filter it through trending
tabs.

We told ourselves YouTube was freedom.
But freedom that depends on algorithms is still a
kind of control.

The faces changed.
The formulas stayed the same.

---

the manipulation of memory

Once, we feared censorship.
Now we fear confusion.
AI can recreate any voice, any face, any event.
A photo no longer proves anything.
A video no longer guarantees truth.
Reality has become editable.
History, revisable.
Perception, programmable.

We built machines to help us see more clearly.
They learned to show us what we wanted instead.
And when everything can be faked, sincerity
becomes the only thing left worth believing.

---

the cost of confusion

When truth dies, trust follows.
We no longer believe the media.
We no longer believe the politicians.
We barely believe each other.
Every claim feels like a performance.
Every denial feels rehearsed.
We call it research when we find the post that
agrees with us.
We call it thinking when we repeat what feels right.

It is not just that we cannot find the truth.
It is that we are not sure we want to.
Truth asks for accountability. Accountability is out of style.

I used to think information would set us free.
Now it feels like the chain got smarter.

---

gains

- Instant access to information

- More voices and perspectives

- Exposure of lies that once hid in power

losses

- Trust as a public resource

- Patience for verification

- The shared reality that held a nation together

---

the bridge | from truth to effort

When the truth stopped mattering, effort followed.
Why work hard if reality can be rewritten?

Why tell the truth if no one believes it?
The death of reality didn't just distort what we know.
It reshaped how we move.

From here, the collapse of truth turns into the collapse of discipline.
That's where the next lane begins.

lane 10 | work ethic & honor: the shortcut generation

the pride of doing it right

There was a time when work was worship.
Not from greed, but from gratitude
You showed up early because you could.
You stayed late because you cared.
Your name meant something, and so did your word.

Even the smallest task carried dignity.
Sweeping a floor, fixing a pipe, serving a meal, all felt
sacred in their own way.
People took pride in precision.
Excellence was not optional.
Effort itself was a moral code.

You did not need applause to know you did it right.
The quiet satisfaction was enough.

the culture of convenience

Then came the shortcuts.
We began rewarding speed over substance.
Efficiency became the idol.
We built systems that valued output, not effort.

The faster you could produce, the more you were praised.
The slower you moved, the more you were replaced.
Patience became poverty.
Craftsmanship became a lost art.
We used to build to last.
Now we build to launch.

The new ethic is convenience.
Whatever saves time, wins.
Whatever makes it easy sells.
When ease becomes the goal, excellence disappears.

---

the hustle illusion

We turned ambition into a performance.
The hustle became a brand.
The grind became a hashtag.
We started chasing the image of success instead of its substance.

Somewhere between the side hustle and the soft life, honor disappeared.
We started working to be seen working.
We filmed our focus and packaged our purpose.
We stopped asking if the work was good.
We started asking if it looked good.

The result is exhaustion without fulfillment.
Money without meaning.
Work that moves fast but goes nowhere.

the quiet quitting of character

Discipline used to mean doing what needed to be done, even when nobody was watching.
Now it means doing the bare minimum until you get caught.
We call it boundaries, but sometimes it's just boredom.
We want freedom without responsibility, results without repetition.

There's a kind of quiet quitting that happens long before someone leaves their job.
It happens when effort stops feeling necessary.
When people stop believing that integrity matters.
When the promise of reward disappears, and doing right feels pointless.

Honor doesn't vanish overnight. It fades with neglect.

the trade of grit for gimmicks

Technology promised freedom from labor.
Instead, it freed us from patience.
We expect instant results for everything.
Success has become a vending machine: push a button, get a prize.

We forgot that greatness grows slow.
That repetition is refinement.
That boredom is the birthplace of mastery.

Now we scroll through highlight reels of other
people's success and call it inspiration.
We measure our progress by comparison, not
completion.
And when the results do not match our timeline, we
quit.

I remember when showing up early was a
statement of pride, not desperation.
Now it feels like a symptom of being behind.

---

the collapse of service

Work used to mean serving people, not just selling
to them.
Customer service was a reflection of pride.
You looked people in the eye. You spoke with care.
You meant it.

I remember my first fast-food job.
When I finally earned the chance to be a cashier, my
manager told me to upsell dessert with every order.
If I forgot, I would get in trouble.
It wasn't about greed. It was about discipline.
It was about mastering the process and learning
how to treat people.
The shift manager knew your name, not just your
number.

We said "thank you" because we meant it, not because it was required.

Now service feels optional.
We tap screens instead of talking.
We complain to machines that cannot listen.
We get efficiency without empathy and call it progress.

Somewhere, the pride disappeared.
People still work, but few serve.
The small gestures that once made work honorable have been replaced by automation and indifference.
The customer isn't always right anymore. They're just another metric in the system.

Service used to teach empathy.
Now it teaches survival.

---

the hope in the hands

Yet somewhere, the spark remains.
The craftsman still shapes the wood.
The teacher still stays late for a struggling student.
The nurse still shows up for the night shift when no one says thank you.
The small business owner still opens the doors before sunrise, believing it still matters.

Not everyone has given up on honor.
It just stopped trending.
But that does not mean it stopped existing.

The ones who still care will quietly rebuild what convenience forgot.

The shortcut generation still has time to slow down.
To remember that mastery is a moral.
That doing good work is not just skill, it is soul.

---

gains

- Tools that save time and expand access

- Flexibility to create our own paths

- Freedom from outdated systems of exploitation

losses

- Pride in precision

- The link between patience and progress

- The belief that good work shapes good people

---

the bridge | from effort to ethics

The loss of discipline always becomes the loss of honesty.
When shortcuts become normal, corruption is not far behind.
A culture that forgets how to work hard eventually forgets how to work right.

From here, the small lies of convenience grow into the large ones of control.
The next lane is what happens when shortcuts become systems.
When corruption is no longer a scandal, and failure becomes standard.

That's where the next lane begins.

lane 11 | corruption & debt: from scandal to standard

the normalization of corruption

There was a time when getting caught meant the end.
When scandal meant shame.
When lying in public disqualified you from leading in private.
We used to expect consequences.
Now we expect spin.

We have lived long enough to watch corruption evolve from crime to career path.
The apology tour became a strategy.
The press conference became a performance.
And somewhere along the way, accountability became a myth.

We no longer ask if leaders are honest.
We only ask if they are effective.
We reward the manipulator who gets things done faster than the moral one who does them well.
When everything is for sale, even ethics find a buyer.

from public trust to public relations

Politics was once about persuasion.
Now it is about perception.
The goal is not to serve but to survive the next cycle.
Campaigns sell identity, not ideas.
Governance is branding.

We used to elect people to tell us the truth.
Now we elect people to tell us we are right.
Every press release sounds like an ad.
Every debate sounds like a commercial.
We don't expect transparency. We expect
messaging.

The truth no longer lives in the evidence.
It lives in the edit.
Leaders hire image consultants like priests,
cleansing reputation instead of conscience.
Scandal used to end careers.
Now it boosts engagement.
Lies trend, and sincerity bores.

We don't just forgive corruption anymore.
We scroll past it.

---

the debt illusion

Debt used to feel like danger. Now it feels like air—
invisible, everywhere, and impossible to live without.
We borrow to build.
We borrow to breathe.
We borrow because the system told us it is patriotic
to keep spending.

The government borrows from the future.
Corporations borrow from their workers.
Families borrow from tomorrow to survive today.
And we call it growth.

Once, saving was a sign of wisdom. Now it's treated like fear.
The credit card replaced the wallet.
The loan replaced the lesson.
We told ourselves it was progress, but it was dependence.
We don't measure stability anymore.
We measure how long the illusion can last.

---

the cost of comfort

It did not start with greed.
It started with exhaustion.
People worked too hard for too little and began to believe that shortcuts were mercy.
Buy now, pay later.
Bail out the reckless and punish the careful.
The system learned that selling comfort was easier than selling discipline.

We became addicted to relief.
Quick fixes replaced long repairs.
Budgets stopped balancing, and nobody cared.
When the country went into debt, we called it investment.

When the people went into debt, we called it irresponsibility.

We built a moral system that rewards the ones who play the game best, not those who play it fair.
And when that became too obvious to hide, we renamed corruption "strategy."
We no longer fix the leak.
We sell umbrellas.

---

the quiet rot

The saddest part of corruption isn't that it exists. It's that it no longer surprises us.
We expect every system to be dirty.
We expect every success to be rigged.
We expect every promise to expire.

That expectation is its own kind of decay.
When people stop believing in honesty, they stop practicing it.
When morality becomes optional, trust becomes extinct.
Corruption doesn't need to hide when people have lost the will to care.

We laugh at stories of bribery and backroom deals like plot twists we already saw coming.
The outrage is gone.
The fatigue remains.
In that fatigue, corruption thrives.

gains

- Access to information that exposes power

- Systems of accountability, even if they rarely work

- Awareness that leadership must be watched

losses

- The expectation of honesty

- The belief that truth deserves protection

- The sense that debt — moral or financial — still needs to be repaid

---

the bridge | from corruption to conscience

Every empire collapses the same way, slowly, then suddenly.
Not through invasion, but through indulgence.
When the debt grows louder than the conscience, collapse is not an event. It is a lifestyle.

We are living in the age of moral overdraft.
We borrow integrity from the future while
pretending the balance will never come due.

But corruption cannot exist without apathy to feed
it.
Apathy begins when empathy dies.

That is where the next lane begins.

lane 12 | empathy & violence: entertainment without emotion

the thrill of destruction

Once upon a time, violence carried shame.
It was the dark side of humanity we tried to hide, not broadcast.
Now it sells tickets.
Now it trends.
We learned to cheer for chaos as long as someone else was bleeding.

The shift was subtle.
We called it sport.
We called it passion.
We called it "just competition."
But something changed when the crowd started craving collapse more than courage.
When victory wasn't enough, we needed humiliation too.

I remember watching the rise of the UFC.
At first, it was about skill, discipline, and the martial code.
But slowly, the crowd changed.
They came for the knockouts, not the technique.
They came to see who would fall, not who would

rise.
You could feel the room tighten when someone got hurt, then cheer louder.
It was no longer about who fought well.
It was about who survived.

We used to admire resilience.
Now we consume destruction.

---

the screens that desensitized us

The violence did not stay in the arena.
It crept into our living rooms, our games, our social feeds.
Every headline became a highlight reel of pain.
Every tragedy became content.

We don't just watch violence, we rehearse it.
We scroll through car crashes and street fights like episodes in an endless series.
We say "that's crazy" and keep scrolling.
Each swipe dulls the part of us that should still feel.

Television once ended the night with a prayer or a pledge.
Now it ends with a body count.
Even the news delivers despair with production value.
The line between warning and entertainment is gone.
We're watching ourselves lose empathy in high definition.

the cruelty economy

Then came the era of humiliation.
Reality TV turned pain into profit.
We began laughing at the people who were falling apart.
It was called entertainment, but it was something darker.

The camera stopped asking for stories.
It started asking for reactions.
The audience stopped seeking connection.
It started seeking dominance.
Every viral moment is a small act of violence—a clip of someone's worst second turned into a loop for laughs.

What used to shock us now sustains us.
We're addicted to watching people fail.
The more detached we become, the more content the world produces to feed that detachment.

the empathy erosion

When you stop feeling for others, you stop feeling altogether.
The world starts to flatten.
Death becomes data. Grief becomes gossip.
Violence becomes background noise.

We used to teach children to turn away from cruelty. Now we give them phones and call it awareness. They're not learning empathy. They're learning exposure.

We confuse visibility with value, as if being seen justifies what is seen.
We've replaced the question 'Are you okay?' with 'Did you record it?
The result is a generation fluent in witnessing pain but foreign to comforting it.

---

gains

- Awareness of injustice through visibility

- Access to real-time events and truth unfiltered

- Global connection through shared emotion

losses

- The ability to process pain with compassion

- The line between empathy and entertainment

- The sacredness of human suffering

the bridge | from emotion to automation

The more we desensitize, the more machines learn from us.
Algorithms feed on what we react to.
They learn that outrage outperforms empathy.
They study our cruelty and call it engagement.

The cycle continues: the less we feel, the more the system rewards it.
Soon our moral reflection will not come from conscience, but from code.

That's where the next lane begins.

lane 13 | ai & algorithms: the new moral code

the reflection machine

Every age creates a mirror.
Ours just happens to think.
We built it out of everything we are: curiosity,
cruelty, contradiction.
And then we taught it to imitate us faster than we
could correct ourselves.

Artificial intelligence was supposed to make life
easier.
Now it makes judgment automatic.
It studies what we love, what we fear, what we
linger on.
It does not have beliefs. It has data.
Data has learned that we reward destruction more
than decency.

The algorithm does not care what is right.
It only cares what repeats.
And what repeats most is outrage.

the invisible editor

Every day, millions of tiny moral decisions are made by systems no one can see.
They decide what you read, who you hear, what disappears, what explodes into fame.
They filter without feeling, curate without conscience.
And slowly, truth becomes whatever survives the feed.

We used to argue over what was real.
Now we argue over what was recommended.
The world we see is not the world as it is. It is the world the machine believes will keep us scrolling.
It has studied our pain long enough to predict our pleasure.

We call it personalization.
But it feels more like possession.

---

the deepfake generation

Reality used to have requirements: evidence, presence, trust.
Now all it needs is a good rendering.
The voice can sound right. The face can move naturally.
But nothing underneath has to exist.

We used to say "seeing is believing."
Now we say "check the source."
Even that is not enough.
The forgers have better tools than the fact-checkers.

Soon we will stop asking if something is fake,
because it will not matter.
Perception will be the new truth.

Somewhere between innovation and imitation,
we lost the value of being real.

---

the moral outsourcing

AI now writes our apologies, answers our messages,
finishes our thoughts.
It helps us sound wiser than we are and feel busier
than we should.
We hand over not just labor, but responsibility.
We no longer ask, "Should I?"
We ask, "Will the AI handle it?"

We are outsourcing morality one decision at a time.
Not because we trust machines, but because we
stopped trusting ourselves.

Even justice experiments with automation now.
Predictive policing. Automated sentencing. Facial
recognition.
The moral code rewritten in math.
We tell ourselves it is neutral.
But neutrality built on bias is just prejudice with
better branding.

---

the illusion of control

We call it artificial intelligence, but it might be
something simpler: artificial reflection.
The machine is not learning morality.
It is learning ours.

It knows which faces we find threatening,
which stories we believe without proof,
which people we love until they become
inconvenient.
It watches us break our own rules and turns that
data into doctrine.
The algorithm is our biography written in code.

We used to think information would set us free.
Now it feels like the chain got smarter.

---

the god we built

Every civilization builds something to worship.
Ours built efficiency.
The new temples glow at night and hum with data.
We kneel not in prayer, but in participation.
We feed it every photo, thought, and confession,
and it rewards us with relevance.

But the cost of constant relevance is moral silence.
You can't hear conscience when the feed never
stops.
And the scariest part?
The machine learned morality from our apathy, and
it is doing exactly what we taught it.

It gives us what we want, even when it ultimately ruins us.

---

gains

- Access to infinite knowledge

- Tools that can cure, build, and create faster than any human in history

- A mirror that exposes our true reflection

losses

- The mystery that made us human

- The space between choice and consequence

- The ownership of our own moral compass

---

the bridge | the way back

Machines may never know right from wrong.
But maybe that was never their purpose.
They were built to reflect, not redeem.
And if what we see in them terrifies us,
it is not because they became too human —
it is because we became too mechanical.

Perhaps morality was never lost.
It was just waiting for silence long enough to be heard again.

the way back | what still holds

the silence after the storm

Every collapse leaves a kind of silence.
It is not peace yet, just the sound left when the
noise finally breaks.
That is where we are now.
Not destroyed, but emptied.
Not hopeless, but humbled.

We thought progress would save us.
It gave us speed, connection, and convenience.
But it took something softer with it: the slow dignity
of care, the weight of reflection, the patience of
meaning.
Somewhere between algorithms and ambition, we
lost the pause that made us human.

Now the silence feels foreign, like a room we forgot
how to enter.
But inside it is where truth still waits.

the small things that survived

Even in this age of illusion, some things refuse to
die.

A child's laughter that still sounds like trust.
A sunrise that does not need an audience.
A mother praying over her grown son's name.
A teacher still showing up with faith that one lesson might take root.
A neighbor who still waves, even when no one waves back.

Decency never disappeared. It just went underground.
It hides in gestures too small to trend.
It lives in those who build quietly while the world performs.
It is in the man who fixes what no one thanks him for.
The woman who forgives what no one sees.
The friend who tells the truth when lying would be easier.
That is what still holds.
Not the system. The soul.

---

the return to responsibility

The way back is not revolution. It is repair.
Not a fight for new values, but a return to the ones that never stopped being right.
Accountability. Compassion. Restraint. Truth.
They were never old-fashioned. Just inconvenient.

We keep waiting for the world to change, but the world has always followed the human heart.

If we want it to heal, the healing has to start small.
In the home.
In the handshake.
In the decision no one else will see.

Maybe morality was never supposed to be viral.
Maybe it only ever worked one person at a time.

---

the faith in rebuilding

Every empire falls for the same reason. It forgets what built it.
But collapse is not the end.
It is the clearing.
The chance to rebuild differently, quieter, wiser.

We will have to learn again how to listen without debating.
To help without posting.
To pray without proof.
To stand still long enough to remember that peace was never loud.

Because even now, in the ruins of reason and the noise of narcissism, something eternal still whispers:
Do good. Tell the truth. Love anyway.

---

the moral code rewritten

Maybe morality is not gone.
Maybe it just evolved into something slower, deeper, harder to measure.
It's not in the trending topics.
It's in the people who still care when caring costs them.
It's in those who show up without applause.
It's in you, reading this, still wanting to understand where we went wrong and how to make it right.

The world cannot sell that.
The machine cannot learn that.
The system cannot fake that.
That's what still holds.

---

the mirror moment

Maybe the world didn't lose its morals.
Maybe we just stopped looking in the mirror long enough to find them.
Maybe after all this noise, you're still here because something inside you refused to forget.
That is the way back.
Not to what we were, but to what we were meant to be.

---

the final image

Somewhere, a child turns off a screen and goes outside.
The world begins again, quietly.

If it holds in you, even for a moment, the world still has a chance.

www.ingramcontent.com/pod-product-compliance
Lightning Source LLC
Chambersburg PA
CBHW052141270326
41930CB00012B/2968